Explo
AM~~ERIGO~~
VESPUCCI

by Ellen B. Cutler

PEARSON
Scott
Foresman

Editorial Offices: Glenview, Illinois • Parsippany, New Jersey • New York, New York

Sales Offices: Needham, Massachusetts • Duluth, Georgia • Glenview, Illinois
Coppell, Texas • Sacramento, California • Mesa, Arizona

Who was Amerigo Vespucci?

Amerigo Vespucci was not the first European explorer to sail across the Atlantic Ocean. He did not lead an **expedition** ashore to explore the new land, nor did he bring back shiploads of gold and other wealth. The continents he called the "New World," however, are named for him.

The European Discovery of America

This engraving of Amerigo Vespucci was made in the 1800s.

Merchants brought spices and silk to Europe by land. In the 1400s, however, wars made land routes to India and China even more dangerous.

Christopher Columbus believed that it was possible to reach Asia by sailing west across the Atlantic Ocean. He was an experienced sailor and persuaded King Ferdinand and Queen Isabella of Spain to support and finance his explorations. In 1492 Columbus landed in the islands south and east of what is now the United States. Confident that he had arrived in the islands in Asia called the Indies, Columbus named the people he found "Indians."

Lorenzo the Magnificent

Lorenzo de'Medici was known as Lorenzo the Magnificent. He was a man of great wealth, a merchant, a banker, and the owner of vast amounts of property.

Lorenzo lived at the time of the Renaissance, a period of great achievements in science, math, and art. He collected books and invited the most brilliant minds of his day to live with him. He hired great artists to paint pictures and carve statues for churches, public buildings, and his home.

Florence was the center of the Italian Renaissance.

The Early Years

Amerigo Vespucci was born in Florence, Italy, on March 9, 1454. His father was a notary, or a person who kept important records. The entire family, in fact, was well respected.

Young Vespucci received a good education. He learned to read and write in Latin. He studied geography, math, and **astronomy**. Vespucci put his excellent education to use in service of the Medici (MEH-dih-chee) family, who sent him on a mission to France and then employed him in Florence. The Medici ruled Florence for nearly three hundred years, and they were also one of the most powerful families in Europe.

A Sense of Adventure

Vespucci was an able man and earned the Medicis' confidence. In 1491 Vespucci was sent to Seville, Spain, and put to work at a company that supplied and prepared ships to go to sea. Spain was a great **maritime** power with ships that traveled from Spanish ports through Europe to northern Africa and the Middle East.

It was an exciting time that stirred Vespucci's sense of adventure and increased his interest in geography. He knew about Columbus's first voyage across the Atlantic in 1492, and Vespucci's company stocked the fleet of ships that Columbus commanded on his second expedition in 1493. It was around this time that the two men met and became friends.

Vespucci helped prepare the ships Columbus (shown here) sailed on his second voyage across the Atlantic Ocean.

Vespucci's Voyages

Although no longer a young man, Vespucci was determined to play an active role in the search for a sea route to the Far East. He knew how to ready a ship for such a long sea voyage. His studies of astronomy had prepared him for the work of a navigator, or a person who plots a ship's course. Conversations with **seafarers** like Columbus made Vespucci sure he would be successful. In 1499 Vespucci **embarked** on his first voyage.

Two Voyages or Four?

It is not certain whether Vespucci made two voyages or four. Some accounts insist he made as many as seven voyages. Information about Vespucci's travels comes from letters he wrote to friends and government officials. In later letters, he added details and changed some of the dates. He also claimed that he sailed to the Americas four times.

Of the four expeditions, only the second and third expeditions can be proved to have taken place.

Systems of Navigation

Navigation is the science of guiding a boat safely from one place to another. A navigator must determine what course to take, how far the ship has traveled, and where it is on the open sea. Today there are instruments that show a ship's **latitude** and **longitude**. In Vespucci's day, however, navigators followed the stars. Clouds and storms could easily push the sailors and their ships off course.

Sailors used an **astrolabe** to determine latitude. With an astrolabe they could measure the height of the Sun in the sky at noon or a star at night. From these measurements sailors knew how far north or south they were. It was difficult, however, to keep the astrolabe in a steady position focused on a star while the ship pitched and rolled on the waves.

Measuring longitude was more difficult as sailing boats often had to take a zigzag course to make best use of the wind. Most navigators used a system called dead reckoning in which the navigator followed changes in the ship's direction using a compass. The navigator tracked how many hours the ship had been sailing and how fast it had been going. From this information, the distance east or west the ship had traveled could be determined.

The astrolabe was invented by the ancient Greeks. It was first used in Europe in the early 1100s.

The First Voyage

In 1499 Vespucci sailed on one of four ships headed across the Atlantic. When the ships reached the coast of what is now South America, Vespucci continued south in search of a passage to India. He sailed beyond the mouth of the Amazon River before turning north to sail up the coast. Vespucci arrived back in Spain by June 1500.

Vespucci halted his expedition because his ship was not seaworthy. Vespucci was sure, however, that he had found the route to Asia and he had already planned his return.

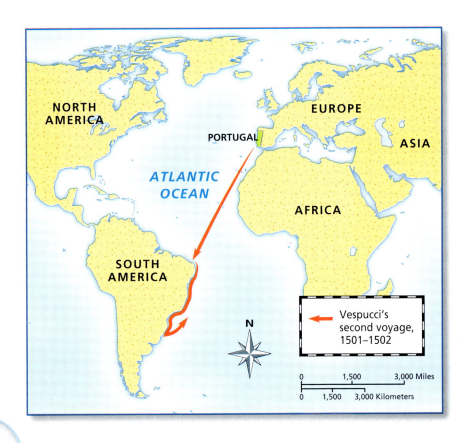

The Second Voyage

The Spanish government refused to support a second expedition. Vespucci turned, therefore, to another maritime power: Portugal. Vespucci embarked on his second voyage from the city of Lisbon in May 1501.

This time Vespucci took a more southerly route across the Atlantic and was able to explore farther down the coast of South America. It is likely that he reached the southern border of Brazil, and he may even have gone as far as southern Argentina. It is not known what route he took back to Portugal, but Vespucci's ship anchored in Lisbon in July 1502.

Vespucci the Navigator

Vespucci invented a better way than dead reckoning to measure longitude. Among the books he brought on board with him was an almanac, or a kind of calendar that lists the times and places stars and planets will appear in the sky.

According to the almanac the Moon was supposed to cross over the planet Mars at midnight on August 23, 1499. Vespucci anchored off the coast of South America and saw the Moon cross over Mars at 6:30 in the morning—not at midnight.

The almanac had been printed in Ferrara, Italy. Using the six-and-a-half hour time difference, Vespucci determined that the ship was 4,800 miles west of Ferrara. Once he knew the distance, Vespucci was able to determine the ship's longitude.

Vespucci's measurements told him something important. The measurements told him that he could not possibly be in the Indies because the Indies were still thousands of miles away.

If he was not near the Indies, Vespucci decided, the land he had found had to be a land that was not on any map. It had to be to him, a "New World."

Descriptions of the New World

In his letters Vespucci wrote that the native peoples he had seen were fast runners and excellent swimmers. He noted, too, that their skin was an almost-red color, "like a lion's mane." Vespucci listened to the speech of the people and decided that each group had its own language.

The people built huts from branches and palm leaves. Some of the houses, Vespucci wrote, were so large that "in one single house we found there were six hundred souls."

The people Vespucci saw placed a high value on things like feathers—"birds' plumes of many colors"—and they made necklaces from fish bones and white or green stones. Although the people knew about gold, jewels, and pearls, Vespucci said, they seemed not to care for them.

The Brazilian Macaw is the largest parrot in the world and can be found in the rain forests of South America.

This is a facsimile of the signature of Amerigo Vespucci, *piloto mayor.*

Vespucci's Last Years

At the end of his life Vespucci was one of the most famous and respected people in Europe. The letters he wrote describing his voyages were copied into several languages and printed under titles such as The Four Voyages of Amerigo and The New World.

In 1505 Vespucci became a Spanish citizen. In recognition of his achievements, the Spanish government named him piloto mayor or "master navigator." One of Vespucci's duties was to prepare a map of the routes ships should take when traveling to what he called the New World. Vespucci died in Seville, Spain, in 1512.

The Naming of America

Both Amerigo Vespucci and Christopher Columbus realized that the lands they had found were a continent and not islands. While Columbus remained convinced that he had discovered an unknown part of Asia, Vespucci believed the lands were a New World.

The **cartographer** Martin Waldseemüller (Wald-say-mule-er) suggested the name *Americus* or *America* in 1507. He was working on a new and more current map of the world when he heard reports about newly explored lands across the Atlantic Ocean. The map Waldseemüller created was the first to include these lands.

Ptolemy the Cartographer

The information in the geography books Columbus and Vespucci studied had not changed much in over one thousand years.

The ancient Greek cartographer Claudius Ptolemy (CLAW-dee-us TALL-eh-mee) probably lived in Egypt from A.D. 100–170 and was one of the greatest scholars of the ancient world. He wrote several books including ones on astronomy and geography.

Ptolemy's maps showed only three continents: Europe, Africa, and Asia. He knew a great deal about the geography

of northern Africa and Europe, so those areas are correctly drawn. Ptolemy, however, had to make guesses about the geography of southern Africa and most of Asia. Ptolemy did not have any idea that the continents of North America, South America, Australia, and Antarctica even were there.

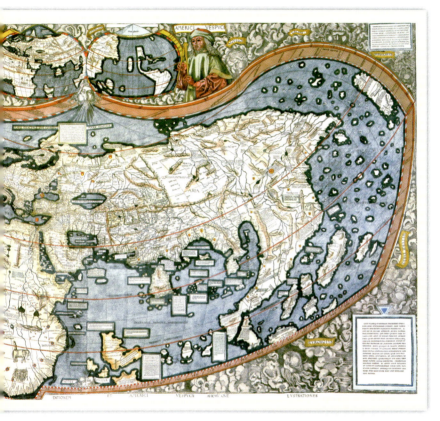

Waldseemüller's map was so large that it had to be printed on twelve sheets of paper which were then pasted together. At the top of the map are portraits of Ptolemy (left) and Vespucci (right). Ptolemy stands next to a picture of his map of the world. Vespucci stands next to a map showing the lands he helped explore. North America looks like a large island while South America is long and thin. The name *America*, printed on the southern continent, appears for the first time on Waldseemüller's map.

Glossary

astrolabe an instrument used by navigators to determine latitude

astronomy the scientific study of the stars, planets, and other bodies beyond Earth's atmosphere

cartographer a mapmaker

embark to set out on a venture

expedition a journey made for a special purpose

latitude the measurement of how far north or south of the equator a place is located

longitude the measurement of how far east or west of the prime meridian (0° longitude) a place is located

maritime having to do with the sea or sailing

seafarer sailor

Exploring with
AMERIGO VESPUCCI

by Ellen B. Cutler

Editorial Offices: Glenview, Illinois • Parsippany, New Jersey • New York, New York

Sales Offices: Needham, Massachusetts • Duluth, Georgia • Glenview, Illinois
Coppell, Texas • Sacramento, California • Mesa, Arizona

Exploring with
AMERIGO
VESPUCCI

by Ellen B. Cutler

Editorial Offices: Glenview, Illinois • Parsippany, New Jersey • New York, New York

Sales Offices: Needham, Massachusetts • Duluth, Georgia • Glenview, Illinois
Coppell, Texas • Sacramento, California • Mesa, Arizona